Ask the Veterinarians

Becky Ward

Dr. Biehle

Dr. Garza

Kewon

Sofia

Kay Gee

Julian

Contents

Rigby®

Introduction

So Many Pets!

A kitten mews loudly as it tries to climb out of its kennel. A ferret runs behind a chair to hide. A little dog barks happily as if to say hello to the other animals. What are all of these four-legged animals doing in one room? They are waiting to see the kind veterinarian!

A veterinarian is a special doctor who cares for animals. For people who love animals, being a vet is a great job. (Vet is a short way to say veterinarian.) In this book, you will meet young people who asked two vets questions about their work. Some of the veterinarians' answers might surprise you!

Chapter One
Pets in the City

Many people enjoy having pets. In big cities and suburbs, pets live in all kinds of homes, such as houses, apartments, and even classrooms. Large pets with lots of energy need to live where they have space to run, so they are happiest in a home with a yard. Small, quiet pets need less space, so they are comfortable in small homes or apartments. People usually choose a pet that will be happy in the kind of home they live in.

No matter where pets live, they need lots of care and attention, including the right kind of food and plenty of exercise. Pets also need a veterinarian's care to stay healthy.

Meet Dr. Biehle

Dr. Biehle has been a veterinarian in the city of Austin, Texas for over 20 years. Lots of people live and work there because Austin has beautiful lakes and hills to look at. Lots of people means lots of pets, and Dr. Biehle treats thousands of Austin pets every year.

Here are some questions young people asked Dr. Biehle, and his answers.

Kewon: *Why did you become a veterinarian?*

Dr. Biehle: I always enjoyed animals, but I had an experience when I was young that made me decide to become a vet. When I was 14, I was working on my family's ranch, and one day I had to deliver a calf all by myself! The mother cow was dying, and I had to save her baby. I was scared, but I worked hard, and the calf lived. After that I knew I wanted to be a vet.

When he was a young man, Dr. Biehle also took care of this pig.

Kay Gee: *Do you only treat pets that are sick?*

Dr. Biehle: No, people bring in healthy pets all the time. When they are about six weeks old, puppies and kittens come in for their first visit. After that they come in once a year for wellness checkups.

During a wellness checkup, I try to find problems before they get serious. That means that I can treat the pet early to keep it from getting sick.

During a wellness checkup, I:
- give shots.
- check for worms, fleas, and ticks.
- look for signs of disease.

Wellness checkups protect dogs and cats from diseases.

Kewon: *Do you ever get scared when you have to treat an animal that may bite you?*

Dr. Biehle: Yes, animals that bite can be dangerous, but I know how to be careful around them. There are two ways to keep an animal from biting me. Sometimes I use a muzzle to keep the animal's mouth closed, and other times I give the animal medicine to calm it down.

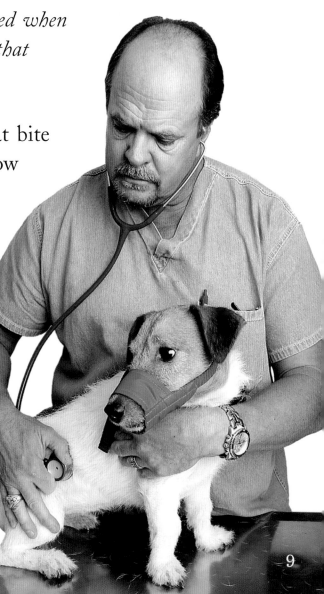

Kay Gee: *What are the most unusual animals you've ever treated?*

Dr. Biehle: I have treated many unusual animals. A short time ago, I treated a camel with a hurt foot and an African lion with an infection that made it hard for it to breathe. Because I work in the city, I also care for unusual pocket pets all the time. (Pocket pets are animals that are small enough to fit in your pocket and to have as pets in an apartment!) Some interesting pocket pets include sugar gliders, which look like chipmunks with very big eyes, and chinchillas, which have soft fur.

Sometimes veterinarians treat unusual pets, like this sugar glider.

Kewon: *Are there animals that people shouldn't have as pets?*

Dr. Biehle: Yes, people shouldn't have wild animals as pets. Some people want raccoons or squirrels for pets because they are cute, but they become hard to control when they get older. It takes special training to learn how to handle wild animals and take care of their needs, so only experts should care for them.

Wild animals like this squirrel and raccoon may be cute, but they do not make good pets.

11

Kay Gee: *How do you know when an animal is sick?*

Dr. Biehle: It's not hard to tell when an animal feels sick. A healthy dog or cat has a shiny coat and eyes that are bright and clear. When a dog or cat gets sick, its coat isn't as shiny and its eyes may look cloudy or tired. Sick animals might also have trouble breathing, might act tired, or might not want to play or eat.

An animal may act and look tired when it is sick.

Kewon: *Do you have any pets? If you do, what do you enjoy about your pets?*

 Dr. Biehle: I have many pets, including two chinchillas, twelve fish, three dogs, and five cats. I also have finches and ringneck doves. (These are both types of birds.) My dog Darla likes to pretend she's brave by shaking my boot as if she's fighting a fierce enemy. I think that this is very funny. I also like the beautiful music my doves make.

These are ringneck doves.

Chapter Two
Farm and Ranch Animals

Texas has many open, grassy areas where farm and ranch animals can eat grass. Cattle, horses, goats, sheep, and pigs are all raised in Texas. These animals are called **livestock.** Farmers and ranchers earn money by selling the animals for food or by selling the animals' fur, milk, or eggs. The farmers and ranchers depend on veterinarians to help keep their livestock healthy.

Texas raises more cattle than any other state.

Livestock in Texas

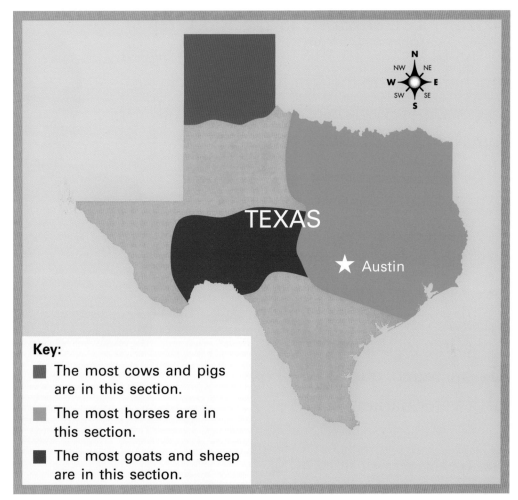

TEXAS

★ Austin

Key:
- The most cows and pigs are in this section.
- The most horses are in this section.
- The most goats and sheep are in this section.

Meet Dr. Garza

Dr. Garza is a veterinarian in the Río Grande Valley in South Texas. In the flat plains of South Texas, ranchers raise many kinds of livestock, so Dr. Garza treats cows, horses, pigs, goats and other animals at his clinic. (A clinic is like a small hospital.)

He loves working on ranches and caring for ranch animals, which is not surprising because his family has owned ranches in the Río Grande Valley for over 400 years!

Keep reading to find out how Dr. Garza answered questions about *his* job as a veterinarian.

Dr. Garza has been a veterinarian for more than 20 years.

Sofia: *What made you want to become a vet?*

Dr. Garza: For me it was an easy choice to become a vet. I grew up on a ranch, and when I was young, I would spend most of my time outdoors. I loved nature and animals, and being a vet seemed like the best way to keep enjoying the things that I loved as a child.

Dr. Garza grew up on a ranch similar to this one.

17

Julian: *Does a vet who cares for farm and ranch animals need more training than a vet who takes care of house pets?*

Dr. Garza: Most students studying to be veterinarians go to college for the same amount of time, but they get to choose the area of veterinary medicine that interests them. Students can spend more time learning about farm animals if that is the training they want. They even make farm visits with a professor from the veterinary school. At the farm, the professor explains how to handle and treat the animals.

Veterinary students learn about animals by visiting farms with their professors.

Sofia: *How is your job in the Río Grande Valley different from being a vet in a city or suburb?*

Dr. Garza: Most vets that work in cities and suburbs treat animals that people keep as pets. I treat animals that help people earn money. Since there are many farms and ranches in the area where I work, I see different diseases than a city vet. The diseases that ranch animals get can spread through an entire herd, or group of animals. I try to *prevent* the diseases from appearing instead of treating them *after* the animals are sick, which can keep the herd healthy and help ranchers save money.

Dr. Garza checks animals for signs of disease.

19

Julian: *What is the most interesting baby animal you've ever delivered?*

Dr. Garza: One day I got an emergency call about a cow that was having trouble delivering its calf. My partner and I went to the ranch and tried to figure out what the problem was and whether we could help. As we tried to get the calf into the right position for birth, its legs kept getting in our way. After almost an hour, we were tired but happy because we delivered the calf successfully. Suddenly another calf began to appear because the cow was having twins! Cows giving birth to twin calves isn't very common, so we were quite surprised.

Sofia: *Do people and animals get the same diseases?*

Dr. Garza: Yes, there are some diseases that both people and animals can get. The most deadly one is **rabies,** which people can get from animal bites. Both animals and people infected with rabies can get very restless and sometimes have trouble with the muscles in their throat, but the disease is treatable. Another dangerous disease is **anthrax**, which is a disease found in soil. Animals can be infected as they eat grass. If an animal has anthrax, it can pass the disease to any person who touches it, making that person very sick. **Mange** and **ringworm** are less serious skin diseases that people can get by petting or touching infected animals.

Diseases and the Animals That Carry Them

Rabies	Anthrax	Mange	Ringworm
skunks	cattle	dogs	cats
bats	sheep	cats	dogs
coyotes	goats	sheep	
foxes	horses	horses	
raccoons	deer	goats	
dogs		pigs	
cats			

Here are some tips from Dr. Biehle and Dr. Garza for young people who want to become veterinarians.

- Learn more about the job by spending time in veterinary clinics.
- Work hard in school because you must have good grades to enter veterinary college.

Visiting a clinic is the best way to learn about being a vet.

Conclusion

A Great Career

It's easy to see that a veterinarian's job is interesting and sometimes surprising. Dr. Biehle and Dr. Garza care for pets and ranch animals, but vets can do other jobs, too. Some vets care for animals in zoos, and others help wild animals that are hurt or sick. Vets try to help these animals so they can return to the wild.

Do these jobs sound interesting? Maybe you'd like to be a veterinarian when you grow up!

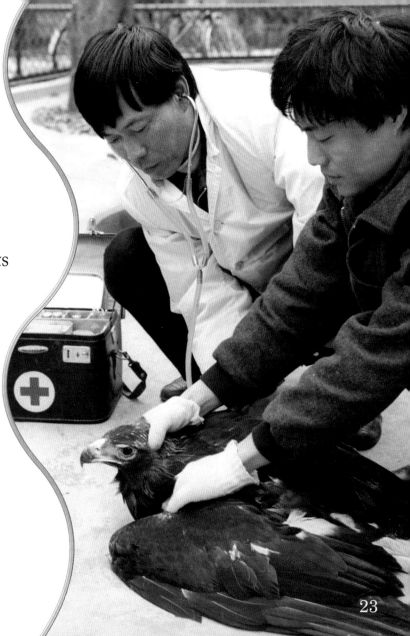

Glossary

anthrax   a serious infection that is spread by animals that eat grass

livestock   animals such as cows and sheep that are raised to be sold

mange   a scaly, itchy skin condition caused by tiny insects

rabies   a serious nerve disease that is spread through animal bites

ringworm   a skin disease that causes itching, redness, and hair loss